Woodland Animals

Owls

barn owl

by Emily Rose Townsend

Consulting Editor: Gail Saunders-Smith, Ph.D.

Consultant: William John Ripple, Professor
Department of Forest Resources
Oregon State University

Capstone press

Mankato, Minnesota

Pebble Books are published by Capstone Press
151 Good Counsel Drive, P.O. Box 669, Mankato, Minnesota 56002
http://www.capstonepress.com

1 2 3 4 5 6 09 08 07 06 05 04

Library of Congress Cataloging-in-Publication Data
Townsend, Emily Rose.
   Owls / by Emily Rose Townsend.
   p. cm.—(Woodland animals)
   Includes bibliographical references and index.
   Contents: Owls—Where owls live—Body parts—What owls do.
   ISBN 0-7368-2068-X (hardcover)
   1. Owls—Juvenile literature. [1. Owls.] I. Title.
QL696.S8T68 2004
598.9'7—dc21   2003011185

Note to Parents and Teachers

The Woodland Animals series supports national science standards
related to life science. This book describes and illustrates owls that
live in woodlands. The photographs support early readers in
understanding the text. The repetition of words and phrases helps
early readers learn new words. This book also introduces early
readers to subject-specific vocabulary words, which are defined in
the Glossary. Early readers may need assistance to read some words
and to use the Table of Contents, Glossary, Read More, Internet
Sites, and Index/Word List sections of the book.

Table of Contents

Owls 5

Where Owls Live 9

Body Parts 13

What Owls Do 17

Glossary 22

Read More 23

Internet Sites 23

Index/Word List 24

Owls

Owls are birds
with big round heads
and flat faces.

great gray owl

Owls have brown, gray, black, and white feathers.

northern spotted owl

areas where owls live

Where Owls Live

Owls live almost everywhere in the world. Many owls live in woodlands.

Woodlands are covered with trees and shrubs. Some owls make nests in trees.

Body Parts

Owls have sharp, curved beaks.

barred owl

14

Owls have big eyes
that face forward.
Owls see well at night.
Owls have good hearing.

screech owl

What Owls Do

Owls catch food with their sharp claws. Most owls hunt for food at night. Some owls hunt during the day.

Pel's fishing owl

Owls hunt and eat frogs, insects, mice, and other small animals. Owls sometimes swallow their food whole.

eastern screech owl

Most owls sleep
during the day.

common screech owl

beak—the hard part of a bird's mouth; owls have sharp, curved beaks that point down.

bird—a warm-blooded animal that has feathers and wings and can lay eggs; owls are birds; there are about 130 kinds of owls.

feather—a light, fluffy part that covers a bird's body

hunt—to find and kill animals for food; owls are good hunters because they have good eyesight, fly quietly, and have a good sense of hearing.

shrub—a plant or bush with woody stems that branch out near the ground

Read More

Ellwood, Nancy. *Owls.* Smart Start Reader. New York: Scholastic, 2000.

Jacobs, Liza. *Owls.* Wild Wild World. San Diego: Blackbirch Press, 2003.

Richardson, Adele. *Owls: Flat-Faced Flyers.* The Wild World of Animals. Mankato, Minn.: Bridgestone Books, 2003.

Internet Sites

FactHound offers a safe, fun way to find Internet sites related to this book. All of the sites on FactHound have been researched by our staff.

Here's how:

1. Visit *www.facthound.com*
2. Type in this special code **073682068X** for age-appropriate sites. Or enter a search word related to this book for a more general search.
3. Click on the Fetch It button.

FactHound will fetch the best sites for you!

23

Index/Word List

beaks, 13
birds, 5
black, 7
brown, 7
claws, 17
day, 17, 21
eat, 19
eyes, 15
faces, 5

feathers, 7
food, 17, 19
gray, 7
heads, 5
hunt, 17, 19
live, 9
nests, 11
night, 15, 17
see, 15

sharp, 13, 17
shrubs, 11
sleep, 21
trees, 11
white, 7
woodlands,
9, 11
world, 9

Word Count: 107
Early-Intervention Level: 13

Editorial Credits

Mari C. Schuh, editor; Patrick Dentinger, designer; Scott Thoms, photo researcher;
Karen Risch, product planning editor

Photo Credits

Comstock, 4, 14
Corbis, 1, 8, 10; Anthony Bannister; Gallo Images, 16; Joe McDonald, 18
Corel, cover
Kit Breen, 12, 20
U.S. Fish and Wildlife Service, 6